Is Gratitude the Most Powerful Prayer?

Is Gratitude the Most Powerful Prayer?

52 Recitable Gratitude Prayers to Heal, Inspire, and Fall in Love with Life Again

SHEKHAR SAHU

Preface

You may not know me. I am not a monk, a guru, or a poet. I don't wear a robe, I wear only questions. I'm not here to teach you; I just wrote what felt true, what filled my heart, and what must be shared. I invite you to walk with me for a while.

In our quest to chase the next big thing, we often lose sight of the gifts we already have. We also notice those who are happy seem to always receive more, which seems unfair. But those who have a grateful heart truly are blessed by the universe with more to be grateful for. Gratitude steadies the mind. It renews the self. It keeps me sane. It keeps me soft. It opens new wonders. It gives more than I know. It heals me and holds me through difficult times. I hope it heals you too.

My first brush with gratitude came through my teachers and mentors around 2016. They spoke often about the quiet power of appreciation and encouraged me to keep a gratitude journal. I began writing in it, sometimes daily, sometimes only when life felt uncertain. Over time, those pages became a small sanctuary. I returned there to remember what still worked, what still gleamed light. Over time, gratitude became my new lens.

A few years later, I discovered Techniques in Prayer Therapy by Dr. Joseph Murphy. His teachings revealed that prayer is not about pleading but aligning. He also shared how holding negativity and resentments affects the human body, sometimes causing physical illness. I began practicing some of his affirmative prayers each day, and to my surprise, subtle shifts began unfolding. A few of my colleagues had long-awaited career advancements, and soon after, I did too. It felt as though something unseen had started moving by alignment. Around the same time, The Go-Giver reminded me that giving and gratitude are twins of the same heart.

I am also fascinated by the work of Dr. Masaru Emoto, who photographed how words and intentions appeared to influence the crystalline structure of water. While his findings are not universally accepted, the imagery stayed with me. The idea that even water might respond to words of love and prayer intrigued me. It reminded me that if water, the essence of life, can be touched by kindness, how deeply must our hearts respond to gratitude?

Since then, I have graced every meal with a small gratitude prayer, offering thanks to all who helped bring that food to my plate, and to the higher power that sustains us all.

If you ever closely look at the food production process, how farmers toil to grow food, and how hands work tirelessly in symphony, it's hard not to feel the reverence. When we learn that every leaf, each bark and every ring of a tree tells the story of how much pollution it drew from the air, we cannot help but whisper thanks to every tree we pass by.

Everywhere I look with genuine inquiry: at how the body functions, how trees and grains nourish us, how strangers in history paved the way for humanity, how precisely the elements, the sun, moon, and planets align to allow life, I overflow with wonder. And when we pause long enough, it can feel as though the rain falls just for us, the snow drifts just for us, **not from pride or delusion, but from connection.**

For many, keeping a gratitude journal becomes mundane, where the same dozen blessings keep repeating. It makes many of us lose motivation to keep it. To help with that, a year ago, I published *Gratitude Journal: A Year of Gratitude*, a guided journal for both beginners and seasoned practitioners. It contains prompts to stir the soul and ask us to slow down. Many shared that the journal nudged them to ask questions they'd never asked before.

When preparing the next edition, I wanted to include a short gratitude prayer as a bonus. But one prayer could not possibly express the vastness of what life offers. Around that time, I was also shaping an idea for a book on awe and wonder. In exploring that theme, I realized that awe itself begins in gratitude. That realization became this book of prayers. No number of volumes can capture it all, but let these fifty-two prayers be our starting point. I derive my inspiration from nature. You'll find most prayers laced with its metaphors. It's a quiet reminder that nature is the best teacher, and we are not disjoint from it.

The world is not perfect, and not every life is thriving. But perhaps this is when we need gratitude the most. These prayers are not written to paint rosy pictures or to deny pain. This book is an invitation to pause amid everyday life and shift attention from what is missing to what remains. In moments of gratitude, struggle begins to turn into significance. Its purpose is simply to help us see again: the beauty, the wonder, the quiet miracles of existence. Science may explain how life works. But when we pause, we realize life itself is a wonder: our body, a moving cosmos of intelligence; our mind, a keeper of mysteries.

The benefits of gratitude are well-researched and well-known. If you are holding this book, you already sense its power or someone who shared it with you does. Perhaps you already keep a gratitude journal, or recite prayers, or perhaps you arrive as a skeptic, curious to explore.

These prayers are written in simple language and kept accessible for people of all faiths and most may resonate with those of no faith too. If any prayer nudges you outside your beliefs, consider it poetic freedom, and move on gently.

Although these prayers arise from real reflection, they are not memoirs of one life but echoes of many lives I have had the opportunity to glimpse, mine among them.

Not every reader will feel grateful for every prayer. Some may carry wounds: absence, hunger, loss, or betrayal. If a prayer feels too tender to touch, skip it. Return to it when your heart feels ready to turn the leaf.

In a world full of longings, most prayers complain or ask for what we lack. Gratitude, being quite the opposite, celebrates the answered prayers and the blessings we already receive without even asking. And imagine, how might the eternal giver respond to such a prayer? I leave that to you to discover, as you breathe in these words and walk this path.

May we discover gratitude as the highest and most powerful form of prayer.

I have wept while writing these prayers.
May they stir your soul too.
May you fall in love with life again.

Contents

Before You Begin

Chapter 1

We will surely agree that life is intricate, complex, and astonishing. So is everything around us. When we pause long enough, we begin to notice the beauty hidden even in what feels the most ordinary. It's from these moments of noticing, like favorite songs in the mind, slow mornings, cool breeze, beating heart, and tree-filtered sunshine, these prayers took shape.

Gratitude is not mere politeness, it's a way of seeing: where sorrow finds meaning, and the mundane beams with light. Let these prayers become a bridge between your breath and the greater mystery.

Some prayers may feel familiar. Others celebrate the gifts we often take for granted. And there are a few prayers that honor adversaries, which in the beginning seemed like a loss or a burden. But in hindsight, we see what they gave us: better opportunities, protection from mishaps, or lessons for growth. What once felt like a curse often returns later as a blessing in disguise.

The 52 prayers are grouped into themes, from morning invocations to nightfall, from human body to the sacred unknown. Yet every prayer touches many facets of life. You may find some prayers echoing among others and blessings reappear across themes. The grace doesn't unfold in a straight line.

Some prayers are brief. Others demand their own space and time. Some softly rhyme, others ask you to pause at each line.

As you read these prayers, or after you have finished, I hope you begin to notice more blessings around you. You may write those blessings in a gratitude journal, and when you are ready, you may write prayers for them. Not everything is included in this book, and many prayers are deliberately left unwritten, as they should arise from lived experiences. You'll find gentle guidance to write your own in the final chapter of the book.

How to Use This Book

There is no single way to use them. Let these prayers meet you where you are.

Read them in silence, or aloud. Recite them alone, or with loved ones. Let someone read them to you.

Read in sequence or at random. Read daily or dedicate one to each week and reflect on it the entire week. Return often to the ones that stay with you. Begin your day with them, or surrender your night through them. Make it a ritual, or save a few for special occasions.

After every stanza, take a breath. Let the imagery sink in. The deeper you look, the more you see.

Use the space between prayers for reflection or to deepen the prayer with your own lines. I warmly encourage you.

When a prayer reminds you of someone, share it with them. When you walk in your garden or sit beneath a tree, read the earthy prayers dedicated to them.

And as you move through your life, carry the tenderness and benevolence in your heart these prayers awaken. Notice how gratitude begins to shift your mood, soften your reactions, and reshape your relationship with life.

Record prayers in your voice. Listen to them. Share them with the world. Be the light you once sought. Become the prayer someone needs. And spread the gifts of gratitude so we all fall in love with life again.

Morning Invocations

Chapter 2

When the Air Became Music

(Prayer 1)

O songs of the universe:
what begins in a quiet hum,
birds carry to the soft wind,
bees pour it into the blooms.
What's your true purpose,
if not to stir our souls?

You draw us into a trance.
Feet tap,
hands clap,
heads groove and sway.
You turn every gathering
into a celebration.

Your lullabies cradle the children,
your melodies comfort the grown.
You wake the sleeping world
with rhythms burning with passion.
You calm the racing heart,

heal the aching soul—
even the plants lean
towards you.

In solitude, you turn silence
into my warm companion.
Chores, study, quiet labors,
and even the mundane feel lighter
when your verses hum
through my bones.

With every song replayed,
you bring back vivid memories:
the laughter, the ache, the scent,
and every sense you have blessed.
The lyrics hold the emotions,
helping me feel
and fully be present.

I thank the ones who carried you,
through cultures,
across unknown lands—
for the beauty they shared so freely.
Language was never in the way.

Your grand organs in cathedrals,
bhajans echoing in temples,
saints chanting in ashrams,
Sufis reciting the poems-
all call the glory
of the divine.

Perhaps the air was made empty
so it could be filled with you.
You are a sanctuary,
a home made of sounds and strings.
I thank you, songs,
the gentle redeemer,
you found me when I needed
your hymn of saving grace.

Becoming the Dawn

(Prayer 2)

O Sunrise!
You return today and every day
melting away the cold,
the darkness and the blues,
painting the sky with gold dust
and ember hues.
You kiss the dew,
glaze each stone,
and breathe life into blossoms
not yet known.

The fog retreats,
and stars quietly bow away.
As my window unveils
a blessed new world,
my heart swells with reverence,
wonder and pure joy.
Thank you for this daily magic show.

I roam deserted lands,
sail vast oceans,
navigate thorny jungles,
and climb up high hills—
for your glimpse,
and your radiant gaze.
Isn't this my true pilgrimage?

O time keeper of the universe:
you've witnessed
my first breath in a mist,
watched each move
and every step.
And you perhaps knew me well
in past lives left behind.
Aren't you the sacred mirror
of all that is intricate,
fierce, and kind?

Your every rise reminds me,
though life is but a fleeting moment
the world keeps churning on.
Still, I must rise to begin anew.
I lay out a fresh canvas
and paint my life
with my own sun,
in a dawn brand-new.

I bow to you,
my teacher,
my first light,
my eternal trustee,
keeper of all beginnings.

Each Inhale, a Prayer

(Prayer 3)

The breath connects me
to the world of invisible air.
It's a thread woven
through trees and forests,
shared by every being
as a quiet uniting force.

We are born breathing freely,
yet only awaken to its grace:
when we are infirm,
or when the time comes
for its escape.

I hiked the mountains,
roamed through the jungle,
filled my soul with petrichor,
each inhale whispered a prayer—
I didn't know,
I always needed.

The breath is ancient
and has no end.
It is a bridge to the divine:
a rhythm, a gateway, a scent,
and a sacred sign.

It dances to the rhythm
of my emotions.
In watching breath,
I enter trance.

Each breath is a blessing,
not earned, but always given.
May I never take the breath
for granted,
and greet each one
turning inward with gratitude.

Gratitude for Movement

(Prayer 4)

You came disguised as play:
in running around the house
in the garden and the streets,
laughter in the neighbourhood,
climbing apricot and mango trees,
chasing the loose kite free floating.
You made my growing up
a celebration.
I missed you, dear Exercise!

In life's seriousness,
I stiffened in the daily rut,
and forgot the fun I once had.
Then I found you waiting:
stepping barefoot on grass,
walking through the jungle,
running on the beach,
climbing mountain peaks,
in sweat,

in stretches,
and in the heartbeats.
Thank you for returning my joy.

In my movements,
gentle rhythms
stir my hunger,
my body breathes in peace,
I feel strength in my bones
and my heart flows
lighter than the breeze.

You are not a mere routine,
you are an easer of pain,
balm to the soul,
a transformer of the vessel.
With you, my life began
to move again.
You filled it with purpose
and deep breath.

May I never forget your gifts,
and always find you
disguised as play.

Clock and Hourglass

(Prayer 5)

O Time,
the most precious of all—
you are infinite
and yet ever fleeting.

Nature and human lives
move with you in unison:
tides,
day and night,
phases of the moon,
length of our shadows,
and circle of life.
I thank you for carrying
this eternal rhythm.

You teach patience,
for seeds need time
to grow into fruits,
eggs unveil life

for ready wings,
clay becomes pottery
in the kiln's slow burn.
Everything that matters
takes its due time.

You are measured,
and yet immeasurable.
You crawl through
dread, sorrow,
and waiting.
You slip through fingers
in warm company,
and in delight—
like the final scene
of a beautiful film.

You are my ship.
You have been sailing
me into the past:
when I revisit beloved memories
and old photographs,
when I gaze up at stars
that sent their flames
eons ago,
and when my mistakes reveal
the necessary truths.

And into the future:
when I imagine
what the world could be,
in hopes that my heart carries,
in dreams I dared

and longed in wonder.
I thank you,
for letting me
journey through time.

I learned the harsh truth—
the future doesn't lie
in our complete control,
and the time passed
won't return.
But it's the present moment
that blesses us with true abundance.
Only living with intention and humility
writes in gold
in our life's book.

And like lush grass
growing over parched lands,
you become our silent healer.
You soften the blow
from loss, grief,
and clashes of hearts.
In time, our soul finds peace.

You remind us,
life is a tender loan.
And I ask,
if that's a curse or a blessing?
What if time never runs out?
Would time be worth more,
or worth nothing?
Would I rise and thrive
or drift in the shadows

of the endless loop?
I thank you for the mystery
you carry—
you are both
clock and hourglass.

May I always remember
your nature of impermanence.
So may I walk gently
as if the next moments
were my last.

Let me count my blessings,
and greet each moment
with none left behind.

O Time, the eternal river,
I may not hold you,
but I flow with you.
I thank you
for every moment
we lived together.

Gratitude for the Body

Chapter 3

The Gift of Sight

(Prayer 6)

I am grateful for my quiet eyes,
which showed me
this beautiful world.
When I left the womb
and the light touched my skin,
your gaze met
my mother's face,
and that was my first comfort.
You have since worked tirelessly
drawing the light for me.

You showed the world
in crisp outlines.
Each form unveiled,
each shape defined:
ant hills,
tiny bees,
distant mountains,

vastness of the seas,
countless pages,
and my own needs.

They witnessed me in awe—
of shadows and silhouettes,
calming blue sky,
mosaic of the leaves,
playful petals,
forever guiding moon,
unrelenting fiery sun,
and flickers of magical stars.

They have closed in fear,
softened in compassion,
and wept for love.

I am forever grateful
for all memories I made,
faces that linger,
sunsets I couldn't name,
every beauty I passed by,
dreams I held in my soul.
I thank you.

Echoing in My Bones

(Prayer 7)

In closing my eyes, I listen.
And I thank my ears
for letting me hear the world's ways:
first words of my parents,
the moment they called my name,
the speeches that resonated deep,
the sounds I call my mother tongue.

I thank them
for anchoring both
my body and my soul,
for guiding me
through torrents and blind turns.

And I thank them for music,
its rhythm and melodies:
rolling waves,
rustling trees,
the wind's roar,

the rain's whisper,
and birdsongs.
Each one, a balm,
has soothed me from within.

Without them,
our world would be quieter,
like a planet untouched by songs.

Through them,
I heard encouragement,
the ache behind tears,
infectious laughter,
voice of love,
chanting of the divine,
and hum of silence.
All voices continue
strumming in my bones.

My ears tuned me
to life's beauty and songs.
How can I ever thank
them enough?

Belly Wisdom

(Prayer 8)

I thank you, Furnace,
you live inside me,
turn the earth into fire.
You take the grain,
the leaf, the fruit,
and feed the *Prāna*—the life force.

You toil through waking hours
churning beneath my chest,
and whisper your work
even into my sleep.

The river of nourishment
always flowed unseen,
even when I had no meal or means.
Still, you offered strength and comfort,
when I sought it as your refugee.

In your contentment,
my mind flows in peace,
and grants me my restful sleep.

I am thankful for the wisdom
that rose from my belly,
for the times I risked everything.

With you, I come from the soil.
Without your quiet strength,
I wouldn't walk a mile.

May I learn the rhythm of restraints,
nourish you in kindness,
and offer the rest
you silently seek.
I surrender to you
in your nurturing care.

Gratitude for Hands

(Prayer 9)

O Hands, my link to the world,
you've touched fire and frost,
flowers and barks,
soil and sweat.
Through you, I have felt the universe.
I thank you.

Without attention,
you scratch that stubborn itch,
carry weight, open doors,
feed me, care for me,
and shield me from harm.
You toil, you build, you earn,
you craft, you write, you garden.
You let me shape joy through
acts of service,
both mighty and humble.
I'm grateful for your devotion.

You also carry emotions—
touch my face in grief and wonder,
wipe my tears,
hold others with trust,
nurse the ailing,
pet my furry companions,
and embrace those I love.

When words can't hold the depths,
you silently gesture.
You've held memories,
both tender and rough.
I can't thank you enough.

My hands are a blessing,
a divine instrument.
I pray with folded hands
and gaze full of reverence.
May I receive and offer
with open palms.
May my every act
walk in the light.
May my hands serve
with truth and compassion.

In Stillness and Silence

Chapter 4

The Prayer Without Words

(Prayer 10)

How do I read a prayer for silence,
when not speaking filled me
with joy beyond all desire.
I always return to you.

When I took a step back
and gave everything a rest—
I noticed my breath,
sounds flowing outside,
and a silent hum within.

You calmed my racing heart,
offered moments of stillness,
retuned my aching body,
and I could hear
my own heart's rhythm.

In silence, I learnt
to sleep like a child,
listen deeply,
cry profoundly,
and heal eternally.

In anger, I chose silence,
in rage, I chose silence.
Many mishaps averted,
regrets spared,
softness restored
by choosing your grace.

I cherish the hours
you stayed with me:
walks among trees,
hikes to the summit,
waterfalls gushing down,
snow falling as if just for me.

I sat in silent devotion,
within your hush,
in night's soft lap,
I remembered who I was.
Silence turned the golden leaf.

All prayers begin and end in you,
a melody from above flows through.
In a world of confusion,
stillness is rare.
I thank you, silence,
for being there.

Gratitude for the Solitude

(Prayer 11)

Silence is not emptiness,
it's full of presence,
where the soul whispers,
and the heart listens.
It's a rare luxury:
to pause, to be still,
to have nowhere to rush.

Solitude is not isolation,
It's not turning away,
but turning inwards
in moments of growth—
in time, in my own way.

Every hurdle I crossed on my own,
I gently began to transform.
In pain, my body remembered how to heal.
In quiet knowing that I am enough,
I realized how strong I've been all along.

In heartbreak, I discovered a new dawn.
In fear of oblivion,
I found the road to divine.

When I have company,
I am truly with them.
I choose the moment,
not from duty,
not out of need,
but from fullness,
from the wish to share—
the beauty I have seen,
and the gifts I've received.

They judged stillness as loneliness,
but it's where I met my soul.
The world becomes family,
the universe feels like home—
I only realized this truth
while travelling alone.
And now when I know,
I belong to the whole.

Solitude is a mirror,
where I met my truest self.
I thank you, Solitude,
for teaching me
to enjoy my own company.

Gratitude for Boundaries, and Choosing Myself

(Prayer 12)

O Boundaries, my guardian—
when giving in was easier,
you whispered courage
to say "no."
The guilt crept in,
but you helped me
stand my ground.
I thank you.

When my kindness
was deemed as weakness,
and I could easily be worn down,
my boundaries rose up
to my rescue.
And they showed me
which plants deserve my watering.

I chose to walk away,
all tender fruits need hard shells.
What is a river,
if not for its banks,
a garden without its hedge?
I thank my boundaries.

I feared isolation,
but silence felt safer than the noise
of a shallow company.
I chose my space with intention,
for my time is sacred.
Choosing oneself was never unkind.

When all others chose
the chaos, the temptations—
I listened to my soul,
for what it needed most.
I carved out rhythms,
and norms of my own.
I chose the path untaken.

I was misunderstood,
but I wouldn't give up
my becoming.
I chose self-preservation,
I said yes to the self
I once left behind.
I will never again
walk away from my soul.

Pages That Held My Storm

(Prayer 13)

Dear Diary,
Talking to you was a ritual,
scribbles became my anthem.
You stood beside me
for more years than I can count.
Some years I filled copies,
some years slowed down,
you still whispered, "*I am here.*"
And when I returned,
it felt like I'd never left.

Many hopes and dreams unfurled on paper,
and you absorbed
all my secret confessions.
Some pages held
sweet memories and pressed flowers.
Some lines were smudged
by my tears.
In the moments of darkness—

you never left me alone,
your presence lifted my strength
and held my hand
through each shadow.
Thank you for safeguarding
my core memories,
my treasures.

My dearest Diary,
our bond knew no rules,
the words poured freely—
some filled with half-forgotten memories,
others lit with profound revelations.

As a sacred inner voice,
you echoed—
life's quiet gifts and simple pleasures,
where I lacked,
who I must forgive
and seek forgiveness from?
You spoke to me
without ever speaking.

You were my first book,
I was the main character,
still held in humility
and our shared ledger.
You've inspired the stories
I've yet to write.
When I read you,
I pause and turn back time—

you've made me a time traveller.
In weaving words, I didn't realize,
we had written a grand chronicle.

You stayed, you remembered,
you witnessed without judgement.
You've always been my gentle guide,
my therapy, my companion.
I pen these words thanking you
in great reverence.

Lamps in My Night

(Prayer 14)

O Keeper of vast treasures—
beyond wisdom,
experience and time.
To have read you
is a rare luxury.
Let me forever
behold your grace.

You hypnotized me
with the flutter of your pages,
your smooth, tender touch,
scent of fresh print,
beauty in imprints—
precious letters from time.
Thank you for blessing me
with your enduring grace.

Thousands sought solace
fearing oblivion,
longing to share and preserve
what must not be forgotten.
You've guarded wisdom
from rust and ruin.

They wrote despite not knowing
if their words would survive
the endless sea,
be approved by kings
and those of might,
or reach even a pair of eyes.
Yet they wrote.
So I thank the authors
for giving more
than the world could ever repay.

And the admirers of craft,
the baton bearers:
readers, librarians, translators,
parents and teachers
who showed us the worth.
And my friend who took me
to a paradise called the library.
I am grateful to you all.

You have guided
generations and civilizations
as scriptures and holy books.
Thank you for being
our lamp in darkness,
our comfort in the storm.

You have been my sanctuary
and my true companion.
In your pages,
I have lived through a hundred bodies,
travelled far beyond my world,
learnt more than my own experience.
You have taught me to see.

You knew what I didn't even know
about myself.
You held a mirror without judgement,
for the judgment be mine.
What would I be in your absence?

May more hearts be well read,
and kindness be their ink.
May my thoughts and actions
echo your grace.
May I too become a book
for someone else.

With folded hands,
I bow in every leaf.

Gratitude for Art

How could I not admire art,
when my whole life is a canvas.
Crayon stains on childhood walls
had unveiled my first art.

You shapeshift:
from pages to pixels,
film reels to musicals,
savory dishes to heavenly gardens,
tear-soaked journals
to homes echoing in devotion.
You melt every emotion,
even the hearts
cast away in shackles.

You are a silent magician,
a savior to many.
You heal wounds,
soothe hearts

tangled in quiet battles,
and ignite us from the deepest slumber.
You are a cry for help,
yet also a prayer in reverence.
Thank you for finding me
when I needed your graceful pallet.

What is beauty
if not the divine artistry?
Who draws more marvels
than the creator?
Let me behold
your light and splendor,
and may you bless me
with your awe and colors.
May it open a window
for the seeker
and bring comfort
to the uncomfortable.

.

In Pain and Not Knowing

Chapter 5

In Sickness, I Thank You

(Prayer 16)

When the sickness engulfs me,
with ache in flesh and dimming spirit,
I remember the blessings,
I too often overlooked.

Even in losing the strength,
this flesh still fights.
Racing heart,
trembling breath,
and cells ablaze
stage a great battle
to restore and repair.
I bow to this war within.

In the body's unyielding spirit,
I saw, it knows the laws of balance,
and gathers the infinite strength
from the universe.
I thank this universal balance.

I thank the allies who join forces:
healers, family, friends,
caregivers,
and even strangers
who extended kindness and loving care.
Scientists and sages of ancient lore,
who devoted their lives
to the pursuit of cures,
proved we are more than mere survivors.

O Illness, you are a stern teacher.
In losing control I realized,
possessions are worth the dust,
health is what I should care for, first.

In pain, days turn slowly,
healing not just the body's ailments,
but also of the soul's old wounds.

In breaking bones,
I learnt to walk with others' pain.
Life tries us again, and again,
yet precious, it's worth living for.
Everyone is weighed down
by silent battles,
let my prayers quietly reach them.

Still, I thank you.
May this season of suffering show me
how to cradle the world's wounds,
as tenderly as I hold my very own.

And may I rise from illness,
softer, stronger
and more whole.

The Grace of Not Knowing

(Prayer 17)

Trembling before
what I can't yet see,
I fear what's coming.
The world carries infinite turns,
unfolding life experiences:
anxious,
unscripted,
yet beautiful.
O force unknown, I thank you.

Though everything appears
beyond my control:
fruits of my labour,
choice of daily battles,
or being loved in return.
It always keeps my pride at bay.
O sacred trickster, I thank you.

I get lost in the fog
thick with uncertainty,
and yet it whispers some secrets—
how to face life's trials head-on,
nourish like a monk,
train with patience,
and forge joy into skill.
You prepared me to change course
when life demands.

What would life really be
if I could glance into the future?
Would I be free
or petrified *with dread*
of all I would see?
I'd be stuck reading
a lifeless book over,
and over again.
I am grateful
for the unrevealed mystery.

What I feared shaped me,
what I needed always arrived,
beyond imagination,
quietly in time.
I now welcome uncertainty,
and its grace.

O Uncertainty!
You are my guide
both invisible and uncalled.
You kept me humble,
and you kept me alive.

And if I look back,
I weathered storms,
often walked blindfolded,
and even fell on my face.
Yet I stood tall,
wore a smile,
and voyaged life's long miles.

I thank you,
dear life's mystery,
for waiting to reveal,
for the wonders
you poured in me,
for keeping my awe alive.
Guide my actions
with your grace,
steady me through
those wavering days.

Falling, I Rose

(Prayer 18)

I stumbled,
I mumbled,
I fell off my bike,
my first words were broken,
my strokes were uneven.
Tenderly, I crawled
like an inchworm,
I know, O Failure,
you never wanted me
to give up,
you wanted me to go on.

I feared you more,
when the pen replaced the pencil,
and the training wheels fell away.
But you revealed the right paths,
and the ones that crumbled,
nudging me
to course-correct,

and dared me
to begin again.
As the stakes of my mistakes
grew higher,
so did the muscles
of my character.

Failures stripped off
layers of my false pride,
stilled the water within,
until my values colored
the river of my life.
And I surrendered
my desire to be flawless.

Every mistake knocked me,
carving deep empathy
and resilience within.
May I now see others' wounds,
and may my mistakes
become their lighthouse.
For I too was guided by
a hall of stars
who have walked
long before me.

In the moments,
every downhill felt like the end.
You have taught me
rock bottoms are just valleys,
resting place for the next,
even higher ascent.

O Failure,
you were my life's kiln,
your pressure became
my inner fire.
Every fall transformed me
silently, in your cocoon.
I thank you
for drawing me closer,
to my awareness,
to my prism-hued self,
softened, at last, into grace.

Beautifully Flawed

(Prayer 19)

I fell prey to society's mirror
and I asked, in misery:
Why am I not perfect?
Why don't I fit the mould?
Only embracing my flaws
broke this mirror's curse.

The cracks on the loaf
indicate the perfect crust.
My glasses reveal
years devoured in books
and puzzles.
My bruises and callouses show
the adventures I embarked on.
My stretch marks speak
of how I transformed.
My greying strands
and inner scars whisper
stories of endurance.

Why would I seek perfection,
when it kept me hesitating
and left me sidelined?
Only imperfection taught me:
I could paint,
I could sing,
I could dream,
and I could be anything.
I learned I would often stumble,
and still, I would belong.

Lame jokes cracked among friends,
off-key songs, sung
with those we hold dear,
and broken strokes
of handwritten notes
touch our hearts.

Uneven curves
of custom chairs,
loose threads
in handmade quilts,
and clay glazed
with the potter's sweat
have always been luxury.

O Imperfections,
I tried to run from you,
yet you are the one
who has seen me through.
I have made mistakes,
I've hurt, I misjudged,

and my words turned unkind.
From those flaws,
compassion was born.

The garden gloves kept
my hands from soiling.
Only when I lost them
was I graced with the rose's touch.
The tiles must break
to join Gaudí's beautiful mosaic.

And only through embracing
my broken pieces,
I came out of hiding.
I laid down my shame,
and found my stage,
my courage and my deepest bonds.
Only imperfection taught me
I always belonged.

O Flaws,
you've filled my vacant space
with unexpected grace.
I am not broken.
I no longer run from you.
I am enough to show up.
I became whole
enough to love, and share.

The not quite right
became quietly right.
I gather all my pieces,
and thank you.
I've learned to seek truer mirrors.

Held in Love and Friendship

Chapter 6

To Those Who Wait, Trust

(Prayer 20)

When I met the furry friends,
the beloved creatures:
innocent wide-eyed calves,
fearless, tender pups,
kittens curled up in velvet fur,
goofy monkeys jumping
across the trees,
mighty gentle elephants,
squirrels with flickering tails,
songbirds bathed in rainbow—
I saw the world
bursting with wonders.

Their love language is simple,
cling to warmth, trust the gentle,
and stay close to those who care
without speaking any words.

When we humans lose our way,
they remind us how to return,
with an anthem of love and kindness,
silently sung each day,
on every turn.

I thank my animal friends
for teaching coexistence,
to live with no hate,
no hurry,
and no competition.
They remind us of our purpose:
to share, to love,
and to live with joy
upon this earth.

May I return the same joy,
love, and trust
I receive from them.
May I become the human
they believe us to be.

Gratitude for Teachers

(Prayer 21)

The wonderful teachers, gurus,
the lighthouse in my foggy path,
I thank you.

You were the first I was entrusted to,
when I stepped out of home.
You guided me with immense patience
even when I didn't know
how to hold a pen.
You tenderly disciplined me,
sowed the seed of curiosity.
I am thankful for your care.

You taught me to question,
to see and to wonder:
from the mysteries of life forms
to the stories of civilizations.
You shaped how I see the world.

You patiently listened,
genuinely advised,
protected me from bullies,
gently challenged me,
stood by me.
You gave me more than lessons.

You gave me words,
with them came
the door to new worlds.
You prepared me
not only for livelihood,
but to live with purpose.
I thank you
for all you gave.

Some are still in touch,
some now speak from the stars.
I bow in gratitude.

You were also
dressed as a stranger,
not my teacher,
nor my guide.
And yet, I watched you from afar,
I absorbed your grace,
and your quiet actions.

In your books of knowledge,
there is abundance.
Decades of wisdom,

resting now in my palm.
And within them,
I found my mentors.

Isn't it love?
Teaching students
who would be long gone.
Writing for strangers,
you would never know
how they did transform.

Humanity only advanced
because you passed it on.
And because you gave,
the world moved ahead.
I can't thank you enough.

The Bracelet of Friendship

(Prayer 22)

I found friends through
shifting seasons,
some grew strong
like hardy plants,
others bloomed
on rare occasions.
These bonds weathered
every storm.

They accepted me as I was.
When I was quiet,
they understood,
when loud, they joined in.
We shared laughs,
tears, warm embraces,
and tender moments
that drew us closer.

Even their playful mockery
forged my armour.
Together, we could walk
great distances,
ready for quests unbeaten.

Friendship is like a bracelet,
and each friend is a bead.
Some weigh heavy,
some shine bright,
some gently worn with time,
and some I lost along the way.
But when the bracelet came undone,
you never scattered too far.
I cherish every bead,
each of them, proudly mine.

I also met friends in turning pages
and mystic prayers:
in books, journals
and even divine whispers.

Friends sheltered me
from the world outside,
provided a safe haven,
my home away from home.
They offered patience,
held no judgement,
some, like stars,
lit my path from afar,
and still showed me
right from wrong.

Some friendships
ended too soon,
yet they left their mark.
My gratitude for them
never dulled with time.

Even if I couldn't express,
and even if we just sat in silence,
each reunion hummed
a soft celebration,
a moment I long
to hold forever.
We never know if it's our last.
Let me take a pause,
breathe in,
and treasure it all
in my heart.

Thank you for choosing me,
my friend!
You stood with me
through dust and storms,
and shaped me
with your tender arms.
My heart bows in silent grace
for every bead,
every light
that held me
in our precious band.

To Those Who Held Me First

(Prayer 23)

I never said it out loud,
I thank you for the breath of life–
the greatest gift one could give.
You were young
when you first held me
in your arms.
And yet you were determined,
even in the uncertainty,
in the anxiety
of what lay ahead.

I was just a small blob
of wet clay,
breathing was all I knew.
You molded me
with steady hands, love,
and often tough love.
You taught me all things earthly,
everything needed

for my survival—
to speak, to eat,
to choose, and to dare.

Only in growing up I realized,
you sacrificed your rest,
your sleep, your sweat,
and even yourself for me.
You wanted me to enjoy
the joys, you had to let go.

Since the day of my arrival,
I have always been
the center of your world.
In my sickness,
you sat beside me
the whole night,
so sickness could never scare me.
Even when I am miles apart,
you somehow always know.

There also came helping hands
from nearby.
I thank you my tribe,
my village,
those who stepped in
even without obligations,
and shared the task of raising me.
You were vigilant,
you provided a gentle refuge,
you taught me life lessons,

you have treated me like
your own.
I thank you all.

You opened the doors of learning,
passed on your stories,
planted seeds of compassion
and values in my bones.
You wrestled with money,
your dignity,
and pretentious bonds.
And taught me frugality,
humility, and wisdom—
which joined to become
the compass of my own.
Your roots with nature
are now intertwined in me.

You sheltered me,
you shielded me from storms.
Despite it all,
there were countless moments
I acted entitled,
I blamed you,
and I was unkind.
I now regret them.
Did I hurt you too deeply?
Yet you have forgiven me
every time.
You never demanded
my gratitude,

and thanking you would be
a disrespect
for your unconditional parental love.

As you have once held me,
I often feel the pull
to parent you now.
Only now I see the pain,
you hid from me
beneath the folds of time.
I can sense your presence
even when I cannot see you.
You also showed me how to
listen to the divine.

May my presence be
a soft return
of all that you poured.
I hope to become,
even in parts,
all that you have prayed for
in silence.

I now walk through this world,
head held high,
carrying your blessings,
stitched into my spine.

Constellations Are Revered

(Prayer 24)

They say, you arrive alone,
but before I opened my eyes,
I already belonged:
to wind, to earth,
to rivers, to sun.
In their sacred dance
my life carried on.

In stillness,
I soaked in the rains' perfume,
and remembered,
I am made from the earth's crust,
and my destiny is the dust.
My breath joins the trees' rhythm,
turning into a feast
for someone.
The same universal current

flows within my veins.
Are we all not woven
with breath and cosmic trust?

In solitude,
I heard the hums
in the ancestral scroll.
Many toiled in trials,
others fell in great battles,
and some measured the vastness
of this mysterious world.
I forged my bonds
of family and confidants.
And I received grace
from even nameless strangers,
who poured kindness
from their hearts.
Like stars that shine bright,
yet constellations are revered.
Are we not brushstrokes
on the canvas
of collectives and heritage?

In reflection,
I saw the delicate web
of interbeing,
like planets circling
close in harmony.
Yet stars and souls
are embroidered
in the celestial balance
of longing and freedom.
Even shadows form

only where light falls,
night follows day's descent.
Are we not bound
by place and time?

In belonging,
my soul swam in the ocean,
joined by rivers
of joy, sorrow, and passion.
I discovered the crux
of shared humanity—
so holy,
so whole.
Do we not make
the garland of shared emotions?

The farther I travelled,
the more I belonged.
So may I walk
not lonely, but gently,
knowing all is connected,
and I am a thread
in this grand universe.
I bow in thanks—
to bonds I deeply cherished,
and bonds no words could call,
no needles could thread.

Gratitude for Food, Soil, and the Living Earth

Chapter 7

Gratitude for Trees

(Prayer 25)

To the seeds that bring life,
the plants that green the land,
the many trees I pass by,
I thank you.

All my life,
the nourishment I received
the nectar of fruits,
oh, how I savoured
your heavenly gifts.

You gifted joy,
with every summer swing,
made me believe I could sing.
The adventures I had
helped me see,
that I could climb
not just your branches,
but life's greatest hills.

I roamed through the jungle,
beneath the towering heights,
where dewdrops clung,
raindrops fell,
and branches whispered lullabies.
I was cradled in the wild.

The soft petals opened,
fragrance drew me closer.
In the heavenly gardens,
I forgot my pain.
It's where the beauty
chose to bloom.

You gifted me breath
so gentle and free.
I realized your worth
only where there were no trees.

You are in my favourite books,
in the bones of my own home,
in the music I adore,
and so much more.

You have withstood time,
seen the generations
come and go.
You hold wisdom in silence,
stories carved in your rings.
You taught me the grace
of life's shifting springs—

to cherish what stays,
and let go of what
has to go.

I hugged your trunks
in gratitude
for your silent service,
and for the nameless hands
I'll never know
who once planted you,
a long, long time ago.
Sitting in your shade,
I thank them too.

O Radiant One

(Prayer 26)

O Sun!
the radiant in the sky,
you are unlike the other stars.
They flaunt the beauty
in the night sky,
but you gift us
life's beauty.
You fill the sky, light the planet,
every sunset is a new canvas,
every rainbow, your musing smile.

With your warmth,
you sustain life
on the only planet
we call home.

In the cycle of melt, of mist,
of drought and spring,
you orchestrate this planet's
sacred rivers and rills.

From the trees and fungi
our food is born.
Seeds reach out,
leaves turn,
flowers bloom
beholding your sight.
You have taught me,
time births wonders.

In long winters,
I have searched the sky,
stood at the windows,
longed for a beam
until it fell upon my skin.

You rise every morning,
you bring seasons every cycle,
just as joy follows aching sorrow.
So in the times of darkness,
I knew, I had to begin again.

Your presence feeds my form,
stirs my soul,
and assures me
I never walk alone.

Standing beneath the forest canopy
I reach for your warmth,
I bow in your radiant grace,
grateful for your light divine.

Each Bite a Prayer

(Prayer 27)

The inviting aroma,
sun-soaked grains,
warmth-filled roots,
juicy and colorful fruits,
every plate is a humble feast.

I am grateful
for the food on my table
and the nourishment it brings.
Bound in five sacred elements,
the elements live within,
and I am one with them.

I am grateful
for the countless hands
I could never shake,
that sowed and harvested
the fields,
that processed and brought them

close to me.
Each ingredient,
a silent pilgrim,
has indeed travelled
a thousand miles.

I am thankful
for those who took cuisines
across continents,
who hung onto family recipes,
culinary artists who experimented,
humble corner that knew
my cravings,
friends who had me over,
family members whose
love language was food,
mother who pampered me,
for all the delicacies
that unfurled joy and memory.

Bonds were born
in breaking bread.
There was no celebration
without the aroma
of spices and sweets.

Each bite became a prayer,
and each meal,
a sacred rite.
May no soul go hungry.
May each table

be blessed in abundance.
May every meal
awaken grace within.

Gratitude for Flowers

(Prayer 28)

O flowers, what do I say
in your fragrant glory?
You are the finest gift,
I want to sing your story.

Every heart begins
to softly smile,
in your presence,
even for a while.
You hold the power
to soothe and heal—
through sickness,
mourning, and grief.

Your fragrance
whispers to my soul,
and in every breath,
I feel pure and whole.
With colors so bright,

your soft light shines,
turning gloomy days
into rays divine.

I sat beneath a jacaranda tree,
where bees hummed soft
in gentle glee.
They danced for you
and sang with me.
And in that moment,
your petals fell on me
and I felt completely free.

So soft, so perfect, like a child,
you teach me to be kind and wild.
You're the artist's muse, the poet's sigh.
Your softness echoes in the butterfly.

The sunbird's plumage
to music's tune,
you leave your mark
in every bloom.
Your metaphors
guide me every day
to bloom in time,
in my own way.

Sunflowers, daffodils,
roses in stride,
in every petal,
I find grace and pride.
In different forms,

the love we share,
one true gardener
tends us with sacred care.

For all you teach,
and all you do,
you have my love,
eternal and true.
I thank you.

Gratitude for Water

(Prayer 29)

O water,
even your discovery
is celebrated as a hope,
a sign of life
on distant worlds,
galaxies and beyond.

Yet when we look closer,
you have already graced this blue planet
with your quiet abundance.
I am grateful
for your generous presence.

A long time ago before I was born,
water was my home,
in the gentle womb.
The Earth and our bodies

hold you in perfect measure.
Such a balance
could never be random.

My days begin and end
with your offering,
it's indeed a sacred ritual.
You flow through the rivers,
into my food,
through my body,
and into my very cells—
carrying life's precious nourishment.
I owe my life to you.

Your gentle force
cuts through mountains,
breaks open the caves,
teaches me lessons of humility
to persist, and to overcome.
Softened, the clay is shaped
by potter's hand,
I too am shaped
by your touch.

You grace the Earth:
petrichor after the first pour,
vibrant rainbows in the sky,
birds bathing in the fountains,
blue lilies in full bloom,
and whales breaching
the ocean's horizon.

Rain and tears flow hand in hand
in comforting land and wounds alike,
in nourishing soil and souls as one.

You carry dreams as easily
as you carry storms.
While surfing
the waves towering high,
I believed I could reach the sky.
And I could hear
sounds of the universe calling—
in the conch shell,
while diving in the deep ocean,
and in thunder
rolling through mountains.

I found peace and healing
in a warm bath on cold nights,
the stillness of the lake,
even in the rumbling noise
of raindrops on the roof,
and the gush of the waterfall
free-falling.

You are someone's habitat,
not just ours to consume.
You remind us,
when blessings are abused,
you return as fury.
May my actions keep
the rivers clean,
in honoring your course
and your glory.

Water is ancient:
frozen in glaciers,
resting in the earth's belly;
in deep aquifers.

You are pure and sacred,
held in a prayer bowl,
in the holy water and elixir.
You flow through rivers
that cradled civilizations—
Ganga, Jordan, Nile,
and the ones forgotten.

You are the memory keeper,
the transformer,
the eternal life force.
I am blessed with all your forms,
for I have seen
the universe in each drop.

With hands filled with water,
I pray in gratitude.

O Motherland, I Bow

(*Prayer 30*)

My dearest Earth,
in my gentle pauses you revealed,
you nurture all lives
in cosmic rhythm:
trees, fungi,
animals, humans,
and even the little bugs.
Those who journeyed long distance,
and those who bloomed beside you,
you have welcomed us all.
O Motherland, I thank you.

You adorn and gild
the sacred rivers
to touch the famished fields,
to fill our parched palms.
In your warmth and safety
life learns to flow again.

You gave me freedom
to breathe, to look up.
You gave me a place
to shape, in your muddy arms.
You cradled my first steps,
and even me when I fell,
you gave me friends,
you gave me my village.

You deeply stirred my dream,
urged me beyond the horizon,
to lands unknown, never seen,
to be more than I believed.
And I sailed on my quests
to know the world,
taste every experience,
scatter the joy you once gave,
and carry your hum
into our song.
O Motherland, I bow.

When the rain softly falls,
the trees begin to rustle,
your scent still lingers,
your songs move
through my hair,
in the land
I now call home.

The world now holds me
like family,
and I find your image

everywhere I look.
Thank you for leading me
on my quests.

Many souls toiled and burned
to build you,
with all they ever had:
their love, tears and sweat.
Many fought for freedom,
and some still do,
for the silenced
and for the forever unspoken.
Some tasted fruits of liberation,
while others became
the seeds.
I bow to all bravehearts
for their sacrifices
and selfless deeds.
O guardians, I thank you.

O motherland,
you too had your penance,
when we stripped your lungs,
dug and burnt you
in fear and greed.
Yet you have been
ever forgiving and kind.

May my actions honor you.
May they be free from harm,
untouched by greed,
and protect you for the future.
May they share your earthly gifts

with those who will call me ancestor.
May every soul
find you in peace.

May I too become the seed,
take part in your sacred deeds.
With humility,
I offer you my all,
I am bound in your debt.
I promise,
one day I'll return to you.
O Motherland, I bow.

Pilgrimage to Sacred Heights

(Prayer 31)

O Mountains,
the eldest of all,
protectors of the land,
you have stood tall,
warded off invaders
longer than history records.
I thank you.

In melting snow,
your headwaters
birth the rivers
to quench the land,
nourish life,
and cradle civilizations.

You wear the canopy of pines,
and healing herbs.
You house the hidden creatures,
and villages nestled in your valleys.

With an open heart,
you invite us,
you let us climb those paths
others etched into your ridges.

On your slopes, we chase the thrill
of triumphs and life's boldest pursuits.
Your summits shift our perspective—
every problem becomes ordinary
when we reach atop,
and every new valley
is a place to rest
before we climb the next.

You dance among the elements' fury:
snow, storm,
thunder, quakes.
You teach us to stand strong
in the same adversity,
sheltering creatures
who seek your grace.

We behold the beauty
adorning your feet:
the valley of flowers,
gushing waterfalls,
and fog drifting with your scent.
All sing in your glory.

You have withstood the test of time,
witnessed conflict,
and trembling ground.
You reveal:

it's the lava within the mountain,
penance, and soul-forging trials,
that raise the ordinary
to sacred heights.

You whisper to the sky,
piercing the clouds,
yet your feet remain
on the ground.
And you teach us
to be strong,
and unshakable,
without swelling
into hollow pride.

You host pilgrims
in your sacred heights.
You called me to the Himalayas,
where sages once tasted
nectar of life,
and found the eternal path.
Your echoes remind us
our prayers are heard
by the divine.

Your whisper drew me
to unmarked places.
Path became uneven,
my breath grew heavy,
my feet trembled,
I asked myself, should I go on?

Afraid, on my own,
in your presence
I became whole again.

You whispered truths
fluted through the pine cones.
Words became unnecessary
and I left behind
the noise of my own.

Forgive us, for the times
we carved you,
abused your gifts,
stripped you of your cover,
and drove away your dwellers.
We were blinded by excess.

Like an elder,
you have been ever forgiving.
Now, may our actions
respect you and honor you,
for all you have given,
for being our guiding symbol,
and the sacred altar.
May I carry your strength within
and conquer my inner mountains.

From the valley below,
O Mountain, I bow,
in awe,
in my deepest gratitude.

Where We Work and Live

Chapter 8

More Than Coworkers

(Prayer 32)

Amid the chatter
and footsteps in the hallway,
I paused for a moment,
and I saw how our lives intertwine.
This place, where I spend
most of my waking hours,
is held by countless hands.

Many invisible hands
slip in before the day begins:
like janitors, housekeeping,
and security.
I barely knew your names,
but I see you now.
I thank you.
You keep the lights on,
the air clean, the place safe,
without you,
this place would fall apart.

I thank the cafeteria staff
for the delicious meals.
The cashier who knew
my usual order,
who greeted me
with a bright smile.
Before my first bite,
someone stayed up all night:
farming, cooking, bringing forth.
I thank you.

I thank my colleagues,
who sat beside me
when I was just starting out.
Times I needed advice,
you were always there.
The brainstorming sessions
made me believe
we can conquer anything.
Sharing inside jokes and laughter,
made my days lighter.

The watercooler wasn't just
for small talk.
It's where we discussed
our wildest ideas, and life plans.
And when we shared the meals,
celebrated joys
and broke in shared sorrows,
I realized we were never
just coworkers.
And when you decided to move on,
your absence was deeply felt.

I am grateful for the bosses
and mentors,
who saw my potential,
rooted for my success,
and in an ocean of people,
you made me feel seen.

I honor you, the entrepreneurs
and founders.
Your vision and compassion
birthed this place.
You painted the first stroke
on a blank canvas,
then handed the brush to us.
You trusted strangers, built teams,
and employed thousands.
Because of you, many don't worry
for basic needs and care.
And we can taste leisure
and free our hands
to higher purpose.

In our great diversity
of beliefs and roots,
we learned to listen,
to coexist.
The stories we shared
taught us to stay humble.
They say colleagues
 can't be friends,
perhaps because they haven't
met mine yet.

To the collaborators seen and unseen,
in shared space and across borders,
your work quietly supported mine.
Although unwitnessed,
it mattered deeply.

Together, we have built products,
and we have built dreams.
May we keep uplifting each other.
As we have dreamed,
may we help heal the world.
You have touched my heart,
ignited my mind.
I offer you my sincere gratitude.

Gratitude for Strangers

(Prayer 33)

To all the beautiful souls
we call strangers—
we come from different roots,
walk different roads,
yet every day our lives cross.

Your smile lit up my weary day.
Your guidance found me on my way.
The seat you offered,
the grace you gave,
eased my pain
on a tiring day.

To all hands of silent strangers,
who sow, who scrub, who build—
your sweat irrigates the fields,
keeps the mills turning,
your labour kneads this community.
I thank you.

To those in uniforms:
soldiers who stand
unwavering for peace,
healers and caregivers
who give up their sleep,
donors who give
beyond their breath,
and even after their death—
you are remembered
and I thank you.

To those in the digital world:
whose code connects
and closes the divide,
whose tools and libraries
made life gentler,
whose words became
my light and compass.
I have not met you,
but I thank you.

To the visionaries who invent,
take risks, and form new paths,
the artists and luminaries
who awaken our souls.
When the world
loses its way,
the teachers shape the clay,
and plant the seeds of truth.
You show us the future
in a new light.
Long after we are gone,
your calling will still guide

our children.
Thank you for the gifts you gave,
even when you never
had to give.

Are we really strangers?
The same air stirs our lives,
the same sky cradles us.
We share the blue planet
for home—
echoing the philosophy
of *Vasudhaiv Kutumbakam*:
one world, one big family.

Thank you for reminding us
of our shared purpose:
to live in harmony,
to walk the path of kindness,
to leave the world more tender.

Gratitude for Money

(Prayer 34)

Dear Money,
you're loved by everyone,
but misunderstood by most.
You are a force
that weaves human lives,
a current that turns
the world's wheel.
You are joy in children's candies,
blessings in elders' hands,
excitement in the first salary,
and victory in the first deal.

You bring provisions, healing,
peace, and time for truly living.
You are an enabler of good.
I thank you.

When you were scarce
and I had to stretch,
I learnt the rigor to build myself,
and prepare for your ascent.
In the hardships,
future looked dim,
true faces were revealed,
whether foes or friends.
And yet needs were always
met with grace.
I thank you.

You arrived in unexpected ways
when I needed help,
and even when I felt undeserving:
in loan, gift and raise.
I thank you.

You flow like water—
with a roar in the river,
and stillness in the ocean.
You slip the closed fist.
They say your blessings
can be retained,
only with the mastery
of true wisdom.

You also teach true wealth lies
beyond possessions:
in love, in health,
in peace and freedom.
I have witnessed those sharing
your generosity:

community kitchens, scholarships
and causes curing diseases.
They truly are grace
from beyond.

When you leave my hands,
may you empower those
who uphold high ethics,
and serve the causes I believe in.
May my spending reflect my soul.
May every soul receive
your abundance.

You amplify one's true nature.
So may I always earn with love.
May my path stay clean,
and remain free from
harm, deceit, and regrets.
May I never be swollen
with false pride.

I am grateful for your blessings.

Gratitude for Small Wins

Today I thank the little victories.
I rarely celebrated them,
often failed to see.
Each one a raindrop,
joined to form a still blue lagoon.

Just as my first words
and first steps were celebrated,
may I celebrate
every little stone I turn.
For these small wins,
I thank you.

I am thankful for
my everyday wins:
waking up smiling
without an alarm,
a glass of water

to spark my dawn,
cooking a simple, healthy meal,
choosing fruit over tempting sweets.

When I stretch my spine
and move to the sun's rhythm,
when I step out
on my gloomy days.
Each one, a pebble in my jar,
overflows with blessings.

I thank the wins no one sees:
how I have been keeping
those tough plants alive,
feeding the feathered friends
who joyously sing
before their flight,
listening when arguing was my first urge,
and taking a deep breath
that stopped my unkind words.
For these small wins,
I thank you.

I spent mindfully,
didn't give in to impulse.
I read a page
from the book gathering dust.
Even in doubt, I said yes
to small invitations
opening doors to wider horizons.
These wins, however small,
arrived with a larger grace.

A detour revealed
a beautiful new path.
Writing words of gratitude
lit a candle in my heart.
I welcome these small wins.

I learned even the smallest moments
can stir big emotions.
In times of apathy,
choosing kindness built new trust.
Laughter with my beloveds
was all I needed to go on.

Some moments made me
jump from my seat
and dance in excitement—
they still live with me.
Humble praises and kind words
made me feel seen.
Ticking off tasks
inched me closer to my dreams.
I treasure these small joys.

I am grateful for the pause:
spark that lit my mind
in all directions,
breath within chaos and rush,
whispers of prayer
that reached for grace.

My small wins
count each effort,
and mark how far

I have travelled.
And when I forget,
may they remind me:
every win lets me stay afloat,
my path is scented by petrichor,
and this is enough.
For these small wins,
I thank you.

The Courage to Show Up

(Prayer 36)

On the days of no spark,
the weather mirrored my heart,
my body refused to rise from bed.
Rain, snow,
and heat pushed heavy,
and yet I got up.
I thank you, Will, my silent warrior,
for your courage,
and not leaving my side.

On the days of repeated failure,
I chose one more try—
not mere repetition,
but after reflection.
Each attempt brought me
closer to grace.
I am thankful for those trials.

When all, including me,
had lost faith,
and my feet were trembling,
I was trusted still
by friends, family, and allies.
I thank you for offering
that leap of faith.

I had arrived at an age
where wonder turned optional,
bare minimum became the norm.
But I didn't give in
to numbness,
and chose not to just exist.
I thank my inner child
for keeping the curiosity alive.
I became a lifelong learner.

I thank myself for showing up,
not once was it small,
each time, it was enough.

Look! how far we've come.
May I keep rising,
just like the dawn.

Home That Held Me

(Prayer 37)

To all places I've called home,
homes of my parents and grandparents,
hostels, rentals, and my very own,
however brief the stay,
you welcomed me
as if I always belonged.
I thank you.

You shield me from the elements:
heat, frost, rain, and storm,
and from the world
when it grows too loud.
After every journey
I return to you, my harbor,
where my strength
quietly rises again.
I thank you for holding me.

Your walls knew my secrets,
absorbed my darkness
so I could live freely.
You listened to my stories,
and echoed them in memory.
Many lives unfolded here
with laughter, tears and mischief.
The ceilings whispered of dreams
without bounds,
and urged me to reach for the stars.
It's where I could unravel myself,
without shame or expectation.
I thank you for letting me be.

When I needed to be left alone
to read, reflect and pray,
and to heal in quiet silence,
I found myself cradled
in your cozy nooks and quiet islands.
I thank you for holding me.

The house turned into my home
humming with my favourite song,
my signature decor,
soothing paint, memory walls,
and the meditative joy
of rearranging the shelves.
The corners always breathe
with plants and softly glowing lamps.
We truly shaped each other.

The windchime sang with the breeze.
I walked barefoot, unburdened, at ease.
Curtains danced in sunbeams,
and I too danced, ecstatic and unseen.
The aroma of my favourite food simmering,
and soft incense curling in prayer,
all have my heart.

You are not a mere structure,
you have a soul.
You didn't just house me,
you held me with comfort.
You've witnessed me change,
bloom, wilt, and begin again.
I thank you for holding me.

When I count my blessings,
you are always there,
steady, accepting and content.
May every heart be blessed
with the warmth of a home.
May every room be blessed
with love, abundance,
and the soul's rest.
I am deeply grateful
to be home.

The Gift of the Word

(Prayer 38)

I had forgotten how blessed I am
to treasure this gift of speech—
to peer into the souls,
to touch the hearts,
to see through minds,
and whisper what echoes deep within.

My first words were broken,
uttered from my little mouth,
could be understood
only by my own family.
I thank them for their patience
and joining forces in my learning.
When I stepped into the world
to make new friends,
to share joy
and express my emotions,
it was only possible in your presence,
O language, my guide to the world.

Language was never easy,
I understood it after embracing
a second tongue.
It opened doors so wide,
I journeyed beyond the world
I had known.
And when I fumbled,
language forgave me in every fall.

You taught me to read great books,
recite mystic verses,
sing for the soul,
watch timeless films.
I could witness
ways of distant cultures,
and ache with others' wounds.
They widened my gaze,
lifted my spirit,
and revealed the kinder paths.

Across lands and lives,
across all of time,
we are woven
in words and rhymes.
The language holds the power
to inspire and awaken.
I too have been ignited by its fire,
as knowledge poured
from the vast sea and the reverent choir.
Each word I acquired
was worth the labor.

Next, we gave voice
to silent metals,
etched our language
into code and circuits.
It freed us to leave
toil and sweat behind,
and helped humanity solve
the greater trials.
I bow to this quest
and those who carry it on.

I only ask of language
to help me pause before I speak.
May my words be free from
harm and deceit.
May my voice flow softly as a stream,
heal the aching souls,
and comfort those ready to listen.
May my speech rise for the voiceless.
May I sing in devotion,
and may it reach divine ears.

O Language,
since I now remember your grace,
you exceed all my praise.
I overflow with gratitude,
for every word is a quiet prayer.

Gratitude for Technology:
From Magic to Matter

(Prayer 39)

Born from mind and imagination,
our curiosity and relentless questions,
you now surround our lives
blessing every home,
every field across the horizon.
You turned former privileges to norms,
impossible feats possible,
magic to matter.

Like an oracle, you hold answers
to infinite questions.
You placed the entire library,
theatre, and even orchestra
all in our palms.
Like a timekeeper,
you store away
our precious moments—

never to vanish,
nor to fade.
Thank you for being our messenger.

You carried the illuminating minds
into the distant galaxies,
peering into miniature worlds
of atoms and biology.
We can now look inside
and mend what's broken
in the body,
use bionic limbs,
and spark motion
where nerves go still.
You helped us walk
and feel whole again.

You filled our days with conveniences
that even kings of old would envy.
Clean water at the tap,
warmth at pressing a button,
and flying in the sky—
you have turned
once a dream into our ordinary.

You connected continents,
ancient voyagers dared not cross.
You freed us from the mundane
so we turn to what truly matters,
and what we must.
Thank you for the freedom.

You brought wealth to needy causes.
Lack of food turned to surplus.
You carried water to the thirsting,
and kept workers from harm's way.
With your power in hand,
we invent without ceilings,
reach into the unknown.
Thank you for joining
our restless minds to solve
the Earth's greatest riddles:
the planet, hunger,
mortality, and despair.

You have connected the souls in exile,
those separated by distance,
across lands.
And you gave megaphones
to the voiceless and oppressed,
to rise with the truth
and fight the unjust.
You are the torch
of hope and justice,
passing from one trembling hand
to another.
Thank you for turning
whisper of truth into storms.

May we wield you
with wisdom and compassion.
May we bridge the gaps,
draw into the light
the ones we have forgotten.
May you serve not to dominate,

but to comfort and heal.
So bless these hands
that shape you.
I thank you for your gifts
and all your wonders.

When I Let Go

Chapter 9

The Mirror That Hurt and Healed

(Prayer 40)

This is a hard prayer. For some, it may feel too soon.
For others, it may be the prayer that finally lets them
breathe again.

Enemy! just the word evokes
strong emotions,
rage and confusion,
enough to race the heart,
and to break into sweat.
Some wounded only me,
others carved generational wounds.
Some of you know me,
others were strangers.
Some were fueled by greed,
envy, and apathy,
others by fear, hunger,
and sheer ignorance.

I bore penance in your war of lies,
sabotage and betrayal.
The web of lies you'd woven,
I spent years untangling,
for my ascent.
The fight turned into furnace
sealing the cracks,
forging my strength from within.
It sharpened my judgement,
revealed what matters,
and what I must not fret.

You held the mirror
with brutal honesty,
revealed my flaws
I'd feared to face.
You were my reluctant teacher.

And you painted a stark contrast,
light is not valued
if darkness is never met.
Apathy births chaos,
yet the choice lies with us:
empathy or bleeding.
I now try to place myself
in other's shoes,
so my actions cause no harm.
I remember what I must
not become.

I saw you burning with scars
and fresh wounds.
Perhaps you lacked the privilege,

grace to soften your heart,
a light to guide you.
Perhaps the world taught you
that a strike is safer
than a wound.
And perhaps I didn't shine my light,
offer my lighthouse,
show you what I have seen—
the shared purpose.

I forgive you.
I thank you.
May you heal your wounds,
as I heal too.
May the scars gently remind us:
what we've borne,
what we've learnt.
In the end, we are simply human.
I offer you gratitude.

Thank You for the Letting Go

(Prayer 41)

How long could I crawl with a trailer
filled with all my possessions?
Still, my heart kept dragging
the rusty weight.
I could only walk faster
if I begin to let go.

House plants die
with overwater, overlove.
Only when I stepped back,
the entire garden began to grow.

Guilt and resentments
were the pebbles in my soles.
I could only walk forward,
when I chose to let go.

Trees shed before they wilt:
withering petals, faded leaves,
and decaying fruits.
I could only bloom again,
when I let go of my attachments.

Hoarding possessions,
clenching people and desires
suffocate life.
In declutter of mind,
I saw beauty
and began to breathe again.

I was in constant despair,
and believed survival
demanded holding on.
Letting go was never giving up,
but an absence of forceful action.
It ended the war within.

Dwelling in the past
paralyzed me.
In letting go I heard
the music of now.

Entitlement clouded my mind
breeding complaints,
dimming my sense of control.
Then gratitude cleared the haze.
My heart grew softer again
as I surrendered to grace.

In clinging, I wanted
to cage the bird.
Only when I let her be free,
she returned,
not alone, but with her flock.
In withdrawing from noise,
a new voice emerged.
In losing my voice,
I could speak to my soul.

I thank everything
I had once clung on to,
for nudging me
to let go.

May I slip off these shoes,
and feel the softness of grass.
May I remember always
to let go,
to release,
in due time.

The Sacred Unknown

Chapter 10

O Activists of All Causes

(Prayer 42)

*This poem is a tribute to nonviolent activism across causes
and cultures. It is an offering of gratitude, not a political
statement or call to conflict.*

When the world turned heads away,
you stood forward.
When silence was easy,
you refused.
O activists of all causes,
I thank you.

You sought the hidden truth,
when ignorance felt safer.
You fought for the planet poisoned,
for the rivers stained,
their dwellers suffocated,
for those stripped of basic human dignity,
and for the voiceless creatures:

exploited, bred to death.
All for the hoarded power,
and cruelty masked as progress.

You planted saplings,
though felled trees outnumbered.
Uncovered cruelty in meals
and far beyond,
sometimes hidden,
sometimes normalized
as tradition.

You lit candles and raised slogans,
marched in the pitch dark,
fierce as thunder.
You cleared the thorny trails,
so others could follow.
You whispered truth with compassion
to eyes blinded behind the thick walls.
Thank you for carrying the lantern.

You went after the giants,
the oppressors.
You were armed
with only your words.
One trembling voice joined another,
and before the world knew,
it had become a movement.

Calling your path "hard",
would be unjust
to all you endure.
You witness the horrors,

lose your sanity,
and hear each cry.
You give your time, yourself,
and sometimes your life, too.

You wrestle shadows alone,
questioning if it made
any difference.
You are judged,
again and again,
by those who wouldn't budge.
And when you cry, my friend,
I see your ache and tears.

Every tree you saved,
river revived,
soul freed,
and animal rescued—
for us, just a number;
for them, their everything.
I thank you for not giving up.

Many fell in the battlefields,
fighting for the very privilege
which now exists
as ordinary comforts—
freedom to breathe,
access to bread,
and power to choose.
I bow in deep gratitude
for your selfless endurance.

You are the crack of new dawn,
a beacon of faith in humanity.
Your footprints bear
the tender flowers.
You continue to inspire
this generation and the next.
My inner rebellion
looks up to you
with my deepest gratitude.

Gratitude for Curiosity

(Prayer 43)

O Curiosity,
Ask, is all you asked.
Your torch ushered us
out of caves,
you nourished mankind
for futures to come.
You are the glitter of children's eyes,
navigating the paths unknown
with only the lens of wonder
and whys.

I was once that child—
I reached, I held, I listened,
I smelled, I even tasted
everything that came my way.
I have wandered so far,
yet carry that child still.

You dared to ask—
What lies beyond the stars?
Is Earth truly at the center?
What breathes beneath the leaves?
What pulses under my skin?
And how does life flow within?
Truth always reveals itself
when we begin to ask "why?"

You are the spark
behind every question mark.
You fueled the inner rebels
to break free of dogmas,
and the silent chains
of old customs.
We began to ask, "what if?"

You beamed through the shadows
to reveal a bright new world.
Seekers turned to books and gurus,
pilgrimaged to summits afar,
and the guide within—
to discern right from wrong,
and truths from the world's
deafening noise.
Every "what if?"
forged a "why not?"

A question left unasked,
is a question never answered.
Let us keep asking,
even when silence demands
our surrender.

Let's never stop caring:
not just for ourselves
but for what lies beyond knowing,
and for the light of compassion.

O Curiosity, thank you
for tending the flames
of our inner child.

Dear Future Me

(Prayer 44)

Dear Future Self,
I thank you for our quiet talks.
I know you often think of me,
you echo in my thoughts, too.

I tremble with uncertainty,
and yet you turned setbacks
into stepping stones,
you've weathered
many trials.
Every small step I now take,
I inch closer to becoming you.

I see dreams,
not fantasies,
seeds you once planted,
have grown taller now.
You watered them

with your sweat and heart,
and laid the pavement
so I could begin this walk.

I am often lost
in bucket lists,
society's checklists,
and lists that never end.
Thank you for choosing what mattered,
for shredding the rest.

At times, it would've been easier
to stand safely on the shore.
You gave your all,
but never gave up.
Thank you for sailing
through dark waters.

Thank you for your quiet labor,
your sacrifices,
and for sharing your victories.
I carry them as lanterns
when I journey
through the dark.

I dream of standing
where you are now.
When I lose my way,
I wait for your whispers.
Guide me back to my voyage
towards becoming you.
May we meet soon with grace.

Gratitude for This Moment

(Prayer 45)

I have been in despair—
dwelling in the past,
mourning losses,
regretting paths untaken,
drenched in resentments.
Only the presence softened
my heart.

I have been enslaved
by the future,
drowned in worry
for what hasn't arrived yet.
Only stepping out of the chase
freed me from its clutches.

When I took a pause
between breaths,
I began to notice
beauty and wonder.

A butterfly adores every flower.
A bird doesn't complain
about yesterday's rain.
Trees don't fear the night.

Flowers don't worry
they won't bloom tomorrow.
Bees don't shy to rest
after swimming in nectar.
And children don't wait
for permission
to burst into laughter.

My neighbourhood is adorned
by a lush rose bush.
I'm greeted by its fragrance
and each blushing hue.
I am called by their birdsong.
I now see, the miracle
has been closer to me all along.

Now, I see beauty in everything:
this breath I so graciously received,
cool breeze on my skin,
land that draws me closer,
songs that cradle my heart,
my favourite breakfast
when I have no place to rush,
my mind that can wander
beyond stars,
the heartfelt conversations

I have had,
and the warmth
of a friend's quiet presence.

I have kept myself from
these moments' touch
far too long.
Each moment, a droplet,
is a sky full of treasures.
I see them clearly now.

Let me lose the burden and pain
I myself have chosen,
leave behind
the dense fog of confusion
and my pride that caged me in.
Let me soak it all in—
this sky,
these colors,
this heartbeat.
Let me fully live every moment.

I thank this very moment,
the beginning of the rest,
the silence in the noise,
the particle in the chaos.
I am now fully immersed
in the joyous presence.
This moment is enough.

Gratitude for Life

(Prayer 46)

On my walks through the shadows,
moments of resignation,
sheer agony and despair,
anxious for what awaited tomorrow,
and oblivious to what lay
across the horizon,
"Why me?" was all I could utter.

In time, you showed me
it was just a trial,
and the ways were
still within my reach.
Helping hands emerged quietly,
sometimes from the universe,
at others from deep within.
In crossing every new horizon,
you drew the curtains
on an ever-grander stage.

With life comes countless blessings:
savors of warm food,
safety and shelter,
musky forest scents,
rivers that whisper,
blooms in gardens,
blossoms in hearts,
beautiful souls on shared walks,
hidden comforts we so overlook,
and deep affection
from those we call "mine."

In chasing tomorrow,
we dismiss life's precious gifts,
held in the treasure trove
of presence.
Infinite forces perform
a great symphony
for the breath's gentle birth,
and the miracle of life.
Isn't life itself–*the truest gift*
we could ever receive?
Isn't life less a riddle,
and more a gift
to live in beauty and wonder?

My time here is momentary,
heartbeat ever fleeting,
and the end,
an eternal truth.
It is I who can decide
not life's length,
but its gravity.

May I honor you, O life,
may I live every waking day
not drowned in regret,
nor lost in vain,
but with intention,
and share life's nectar
entrusted to me,
for I am here,
a mere custodian.

In Every Surrender, You Held Me

(Prayer 47)

I missed my turn,
lost, I couldn't retrace,
but still wandered on.
I surrendered to the unknown,
and on the longer road,
I discovered a hidden detour,
beautiful and mine.

What seemed like a failure,
became the new
pass through the mountain.
I surrendered to time,
and its mystery revealed plans
grander than I dared to design.

When my mind was overwhelmed,
indecision kept caving in.
I surrendered to sleep

into the calm of a lake.
Buried beneath,
I discovered a gold mine.

In losing control,
the fear crept in.
I surrendered to breath,
for a river does not decide its course,
and water does not shape itself,
the mountains carve its form.

I chased every deadline,
pushed every key,
burnt the midnight oil.
When every resource was exhausted,
I surrendered to the wisdom—
higher than mere doing.
Water only carries us
when we stop resisting
its flow.

I bow to every surrender.
Each time my actions failed,
you held me
with ease and grace.
Were you waiting for me
all along?

May I always remember,
after every doing,
after my *karma*,
comes the time for surrender.

Nightfall and Return

Chapter 11

Gratitude for Sleep

(Prayer 48)

In growing up I realized,
sleep is the sweetest gift.
After the day's labour,
I truly enjoy
my deep slumber.

Turning the light dim,
I tuck into my cozy bed,
surrounded by soft pillows,
wrapped in my favourite duvet,
in the hush of night and crickets,
I prepare for the sacred comfort.
O sleep you are my gentle keeper.

My body heals in your arms,
my mind rejuvenates.
I have often taken you for granted,
I realised in the nights
my mind wandered

but you were found nowhere.
On holidays, I press snooze,
and I steal a few moments
of your pure luxury.

You come with a whisper
when my mind is lost in chaos
to release the weight,
to forgive,
to forget—
what no longer matters,
what I need not regret.

Every sleep is a moment
of surrender,
I let go of guilt,
and weights of sorrow.
Not that life gets easier,
but I rise stronger.

In dreams, I sail to a new world,
where nothing is impossible,
and no joy out of reach.
It's a reminder to wake up
to the new dawn
and live life as a gift.

When time comes for final sleep,
may I be graced with lullabies
of the universe,
may I be ready open-hearted

to rise freer,
inside a new self.
I thank you, sweet sleep.

Land Beyond Sleep

(Prayer 49)

Every night, in my sleep,
a movie softly unfolds
just for me.
I once ran to a land
with no bounds,
no matter how far
I drifted on.
It showed me the known,
and all I hadn't yet seen,
a universe I now call my own.

Thank you, Dream,
for showing my hidden desires,
what I had longed for,
but I believed I could never aspire.
I am the center of my universe,
it's written in gold
in last night's verse.

In dreams, mystics and thinkers
perfect their craft,
swimming in its creative ocean,
unlocking treasures
of hidden wisdom inside.
O Dream, you have been
the most faithful muse.

In tossing and turning,
I reach for a dream.
You call my mind and body
to return and heal.
You prod the wounds
I've yet to mend,
I turn within,
and the blossoming
of truth begins.

In your shelter,
I released my weight,
dusted the corners
where pain once stayed.
And you echoed a message
to my waking dreams—
to keep the head high,
and believe I could reach any dream.

I once fell from the sky,
scared,
woke in a gasp,
but I was alright.
Nightmares unravel
my unresolved emotions,

like chess puzzles,
replaying my lost battles.
And so I return stronger,
ready to fight any battle.

Each lucid dream I journal,
opens a door to joy and wonder.
And when it's time
for the eternal sleep,
ready I'll be,
having fully lived.

Thank you, Dream,
for your nightly gifts,
for all you've shown,
and the mystery unknown.

Borrowed Light, Endless Blessing

(Prayer 50)

You are every artist's muse,
loved by wanderers, seekers,
and the lost.
You ink the rhymes,
color the canvas,
carry the night,
and in a hush,
fill my heart.
O Moonlight,
let me behold you forever.

You borrow light,
yet you bless the world.
Lit by sun's fierce force,
you paint the night sky
with luster.
O Moon, like you churn breeze
from trials of fire,

you teach me to face adversity,
and radiate calm
from my inner pyres.

You walked with me
through sleepless nights—
garden trails, empty streets,
and ruminating flights.
I once saw you kiss the ocean,
the waves danced
like simmering silver,
I was unready
to part from that moment.
When I drifted into sleep,
you found me still,
through cracks in the window,
through wounds in my soul.

Some of your phases
make me mourn.
But what is lost
will bloom again
with a crescent moon.
You pull the tides,
you have pulled me too.
May I find your grace
in your every return.

O Moon,
may I shine as
effortlessly as you.

May I reflect love
even when I'm in parts
just as you.

The Final Caravan

(Prayer 51)

This prayer is a reflection on the mystery of natural passing.
It is a reminder to live, love, and forgive while we can.
If you're feeling emotionally overwhelmed, please pause and
talk to someone you trust.

You arrived first
when we were just children,
with the passing of someone elderly
and so dear,
enveloped in flowers
and white coffin,
the house hazed with incense,
echoing sobs and hymns.
We were made to believe
you came with
our maker's invitation.

My heart was tender as a bud,
but with years behind me now,
O Death,

will I ever know your purpose?
As the ashes sifted to the Earth,
and fog cleared from my senses,
I learnt the bitter truth—
they never return.

They left their imprints,
but the pyre is still
embered in grief.
After beholding this sheer pain
for the departed,
I know, Death,
you have wept too.

O Death, you are ever feared
and seen through the clouded lens.
You are the river's master,
captain of the ship,
ferrying us from
one home to another,
one veil to the unveiling,
worn vessel to a new womb.
This caravan only camps here
until my time is due.

On every stopover,
my soul was welcomed
into new arms—
a family, an abode of love.
They celebrated my birth
with songs,
as a blessing from the Divine.
They bathed me in more love

than my soul could ever hold.
And I could only give back
by weaving joy
into their living tales.

We live as if death were a myth,
parading as invincibles.
Your subtle hints of the date
unnerve me now.
Is my soul prepared
or still buried in the gardens
I never tended?
Have I stepped past my fears?
Have I asked for forgiveness?
Have I spilled
all I ever longed to say?
Urgency stirs my soul now
from the depths of my slumber.

O Death, forgive me
for I misread you.
I even cursed you.
Death and birth
were never opposites
but secret imposters.
Now that I see you,
may I learn to live fully,
may I love deeply.
And when it's time,
may my departure rise
as a joyful celebration,
echoing my first breath.

When you arrive,
let my soul shed
its past karmic debts,
may I be free of all regrets,
and may my heart soften
in life's quiet reverence.
May I still the waters of my soul,
and we shall meet
at the shore
with life's eternal grace.
Until then, may I live
with open palms and reverence.

O Divine, I Thank You

(Prayer 52)

O Divine!
What could I sing in your praise,
when all things begin
and end in you?
My words could only aspire,
in humility,
to describe the water's taste,
return a leaf to the forest floor,
light a torch before the blazing sun,
or drop a grain into the vastness
of the ocean.

O God,
we seek you in many forms,
and you flow through the formless.
We call you by a thousand names,
yet you hear us in silence,
even before voicing,
even with no words.

We cross hills and deserts
in search of you,
reading holy words,
chanting your names,
singing tales in devotion.

Like a beautiful perfume
that fills my heart
with no flowers in sight,
I feel your constant presence
all around me,
wherever I go.
I thank you
for always walking beside me.

You blessed us with gift of life
and all that sustains.
You gave us breath,
trees to nourish,
and seasons to cleanse.
You surrounded us
with beauty and wonder:
the earth for our home,
stars for guidance,
and flowers to melt our hearts.
And you breathed virtues
into our souls.
Thank you
for making us their custodian.

All things, every inch,
move at your command,
yet you granted us free-will.

In every wrong turn
I wandered lost.
Fear and guilt crept in,
my heart wrenched,
and I froze in place.
Still, your mercy found me
with a chance to begin again.
You showed us the compass
to find right from wrong.
I thank you
for guiding me home.

I dreamed of horizons
greater than I dared to cross.
Wasn't it your grace
that created that spark?
As I took my first steps,
I found new doors,
unexpected and wide open,
and no dreams appeared
distant any longer.
For every closed door,
you revealed one new
grander than before.
Thank you for tending
the garden of my dreams.

You created provisions,
and safe shelters.
You blessed me with sunshine
and joyous moments.
And I also walked
the path of failure,

loss and hardships.
Wasn't it your way
to forge me through the trial,
so I could rise stronger
and wiser again?
Just as the seasons turn,
those storms faded in time.
Thank you for leading me
out of the dark.

You graciously created
worldly pleasures,
I devoured them all.
But when I tasted
your divine bliss,
my tongue repelled
everything else.
You taught me patience,
and strength in restraint.
I thank you
for all the extravagance
you poured without excess.

I have complained,
called you in despair.
I questioned you,
doubted your existence.
I saw the world crumble.
How could you allow
this world to suffer?
You revealed no plan,
perhaps to bear penance
for our past debts.

You lead us
onto the virtuous paths,
to lift from those burdens,
to rise freer
to receive new grace.
I thank you
for your forgiveness,
you never turned me away.

You never did once,
let go of our hands.
O Mother Divine,
I know you rejoice
in our victories.
And in our sufferings,
you weep too.
I thank you
for watching over us
with your motherly gaze.

You see the past
and all yet to unfold.
You reveal just enough
for the wonder to hold.
You nudge me
to take the first step,
in faith,
in your quiet presence.
I have felt you intervene
to steer my feet away
from the thorns.
I see your sign every day,

I hear it in the prayers,
I see it in the moon,
I feel it in the wind.

O Divine Gardener,
you blessed us
with the power to feel:
to share joys,
to ache with others' wounds.
to sprinkle fragrance
in every soul.
With those came
love of our family,
warmth of our friends,
and the kindness of strangers.
Thank you
for harmonizing every hue.

Your generosity
fills hands that serve:
for fighting hunger,
in curing diseases,
gentle words
that heal the weary.
I see your imprint
gleaming in them.
Thank you for tending us
through them.

In pause, in breath,
in closed eyes,
I began to count
these blessings.

Words fell short,
for my heart overflowed
with deepest reverence.
You gave without asking.
I bow to you.

May every soul taste
your grace.
May they witness
your divine presence.
May they realize
you have always been
answering prayers.

May you keep guiding us
on the right path.
May we rise with love
and truthfulness.
May we remember
we come from
your ocean of grace.
With folded hands,
open heart,
and raised chin,
O Divine Eternal, I thank you.

Create Your Own Gratitude Prayer

Chapter 12

Why Create One?

Now that you have gone through the 52 gratitude prayers across themes, some may have touched you deeply. Perhaps you even highlighted your favorite lines. You can continue to read and recite these prayers daily, or return to them on life events and special occasions. Although I tried to make the prayers as inclusive as possible, some parts may not resonate with you. They may not echo your lived experience, or the metaphors may feel unfamiliar. Some prayers were left unwritten on purpose, so you could write your own. Because prayers rooted in your lived experience carry the most power.

The blank pages ahead are waiting for you to create prayers for your parents, guardians, grandparents, neighbours, your city, school, or the life events. If you have a partner, children, or any friend you deeply cherish, you can write prayers for them too.

Tips for Writing Prayers

There are no rules. Your prayer does not have to be perfect, polished, or poetic. It only needs to echo your reverent heart.

Since gratitude shines brightest through details, include concrete moments. You may add your lived stories, your sensory memories, and your inner dialogues.

You may write as collections of phrases, a reflective essay, a poem, or a simple letter. Later in the chapter, I share a few templates you may use as a guide. But feel free to go freeform. If your prayer grows too long, break it into smaller parts and give yourself space to breathe.

If you are writing a prayer for someone, address them directly. It will make it more soulful and intimate. If the prayer is for an object, a feeling, or a force of nature, personifying can bring it alive.

You may also borrow phrases from the prayers in this book, weaving them across themes if you want to create a universal prayer.

Remember, your prayers are living, breathing invocations. Revise them as often as they ask. Read them aloud. Write as if no one else will ever read them, that is when the rawest and truest gratitude emerges to the surface.

Let your prayer find its voice.

Template

Here are three sample structures to help you begin:

Template #1 Movement or Transformation
Gratitude – I thank you for
Realization – I learnt that / You showed me that
Blessing – May I [do / become]

Template #2 Ode
Address – O / Dear
Action – You [did / do] / Something happened
Reflection – I [did / do / felt / learned]
Gratitude – Thank you for [blessing / teaching / holding]

Template #3 Then and Now
Contrast – I once didn't [see / appreciate] you in [difficulty / complaints], but now I do.
Shift – I wanted [X], but now I appreciate [delayed X / what came instead]
Transformation – You shaped me / I was [transformed / forged / shielded]

Closing Blessing

If you have made this far,
I thank you for walking with me.
It's not the end,
but only a beginning.
May the reverence
always linger in your heart.
May you navigate towards the light
of hope and river of grace.

May you return
to these prayers as home.
May they echo with joy
as the pages turn.
May your soul sway gently
in silent remembrance.

Dear Soul, remember,
you have the power
to mend and light your way;
to heal and inspire
the self
and others along the way.

May you become
a lantern in others' storms.
May you guide them home.
May you reveal to them,
the gifts and wonders
we too had once forgotten.
May your words and actions
become the very blessings
you once sought.

May gratitude become
your way of life.
May your life whisper
of a living prayer.
May we meet the universe
with grace.
I thank you
for choosing gratitude.

—Shekhar

Also by the Author

Gratitude Journal: A Year of Gratitude
A 150-prompt, year-long companion to reflect, appreciate, and grow in abundance.
A gentle beginning before these prayers were born.

Available on Amazon
Worldwide:
https://www.amazon.com/dp/B0DRSWX1WN
India:
https://www.amazon.in/dp/B0DYDC989R

Made in the USA
Las Vegas, NV
18 November 2025

34692727R00129